Original title:
Among the Alder Leaves

Copyright © 2025 Creative Arts Management OÜ
All rights reserved.

Author: Charles Whitfield
ISBN HARDBACK: 978-1-80567-352-1
ISBN PAPERBACK: 978-1-80567-651-5

The Leafy Archive of Time

In the woods, where secrets hide,
A squirrel misplaced his nuts with pride.
He laughed as he dug a hole too deep,
Building a treasure, though no one would peep.

The leaves giggled, flapping like fans,
Murmuring jokes, forming leafy bands.
'Time flies,' they chirped, 'like birds on a wire,
But lost nuts make for a great campfire!'

Hymn of the Whispering Woods

A chipmunk crooned to an audience rare,
His tiny voice squeaked through the air.
The trees leaned closer, ear to the ground,
As the critters gathered, their laughter unbound.

One branch declared, 'I'm multi-talented!'
'Can bend and sway, and still be elegant!'
The rustling leaves, in jovial cheer,
Joined in the chorus, 'We're all pioneers!'

Footprints in the Underbrush

A snail with swagger, dressed in a shell,
Slid down a trail, where the wild things dwell.
With every slow move, a dance to impress,
'Look at me shine, look at me mess!'

The ants held a rally, a march full of dreams,
With tiny banners and high-pitched screams.
'What's that on your shoe?' one of them mocked,
'It's not dirt; it's just a leaf that got locked!'

The Art of Stillness in Green

A frog in repose, struck a thoughtful pose,
Contemplated life as it journeyed close.
He croaked out a quip, with a wink of a grin,
'Why hop through a bog when you can just swim?'

The bushes collaborated, their leaves all a-flutter,
'Why rush at all? Just enjoy the clutter.'
With each lazy tick, the sun started to melt,
Even lazy critters deserved to be felt.

Lullabies of the Woodland Realm

In the hush of darkened trees,
Squirrels jump with joyful ease.
Raccoons dance a wild jive,
While owls hoot, 'It's alive!'

Beneath the moonlit, silver beams,
Frogs croak out their silly dreams.
Crickets tap with all their might,
Singing songs to the night.

Hidden Paths of the Earthen Realm

Footpaths twist like a silly grin,
With mushrooms hiding where they've been.
A hedgehog slips in a grand parade,
Waving leaves like a grand charade.

The flowers giggle, shaking bright,
As caterpillars start a fight.
"I'm a butterfly!" they proudly claim,
While they wobble in a leafy game.

An Ode to Nature's Cloister

In a nook where shadows sway,
Bunnies hold their feathery bay.
They play hide and seek with glee,
While bees buzz tunes, oh-so-free!

The breezes swirl with secret plans,
Tickling the tiny flower fans.
As squirrels plot and giggle near,
Nature's stage is full of cheer.

Memories Woven in Roots

Roots are tangled like old friends,
Sharing tales as the day ends.
A wise old tree drops a leaf,
"Take this bit for your belief!"

The shadows dance with grinning glee,
As ants march off to tea party.
Laughter rings through the rustling grass,
With whispers of the vines that pass.

Whispers of the Dappled Light

In the breeze, the shadows play,
Twirling leaves on their merry way.
Squirrels chatter, a comic scene,
A dance of nature, so serene.

Sunbeams tickle the forest floor,
While worms wiggle, seeking more.
Frogs croak jokes in a puddled jest,
In the green, they're truly blessed.

A rabbit hops with a floppy ear,
Wearing a hat, it sounds sincere.
Laughter echoes through the trees,
Nature's laughter carried by the breeze.

Ephemeral Moments in Green

Frogs in tuxedos, quite a sight,
Croak their plans for a late-night flight.
The leaves giggle at each small blunder,
As ants march proudly, always under.

Clouds drift by like fluffy sheep,
While bugs check off their dreams - a leap!
Against the rays, they spin and twirl,
In this green world, laughter swirls.

The daisies wear their brightest hues,
Throwing shade on old-fashioned blues.
Nature's jesters, in colors bright,
Bring joy and laughter, pure delight.

Nature's Cradle of Mystery

In a nook, the mushrooms grin,
Sharing secrets, yet to begin.
Wanderers peek with a fumble,
As sleepy bugs partake in a jumble.

The wind tells tales of days gone past,
Where time drifts slow, yet moments fast.
A hedgehog dons a tiny crown,
Ruling over the haye and brown.

Chirping birds assemble for fun,
In a flash, they burst, then they run.
Misfit squirrels dive from trees,
Their acrobatics sure to please.

The Rhythm of Rustic Rains

Pitter-patter, the raindrops sing,
A tap dance party, a soggy fling.
The puddles form a stage for frogs,
As they leap like dancing dogs.

The trees sway, sharing a joke,
While puddles splash with every poke.
Mice skedaddle from leaf to leaf,
In a rainy game, beyond belief.

Raccoons chatter under the sun,
Plotting mischief, oh what fun!
Nature giggles, a silly refrain,
In the rhythm of this jovial rain.

Poetry of the Pathways

A squirrel tried to steal my hat,
It wore it like a fancy mat.
Each step I took, it danced away,
So much for hats on sunny day.

The path was littered with mud pies,
I navigated those with sighs.
But laughter bubbled from my feet,
I slipped, fell down, and met a beet.

The trees leaned in with gossip low,
About the antics of a crow.
It swooped and dived, a boisterous sight,
Chasing shadows, taking flight.

Twisted roots became my stage,
Where I performed my best rampage.
Each step a story yet to spin,
Nature's playground, let's begin!

The Breath of Nature's Haven

In the garden, I found a cat,
Wearing shades and looking flat.
It posed like a summer star,
While ants marched by in a bizarre car.

Breezes whispered silly tales,
Of chipmunks sailing on toy gales.
A ladybug hosted a tea,
With petals and crumbs for all to see.

A frog tried to start a band,
While bees danced in perfect strand.
Their buzzing notes were quite absurd,
Even the flowers laughed, unheard.

Every leaf a joker's mask,
Nature's comedy, quite the task.
I chuckled as I walked along,
In this haven, where I belong!

Dappled Dreams and Whispered Wishes

In light that tickles through the trees,
A rabbit shouted, "Catch the breeze!"
With every hop, it felt so grand,
Inventing games on leafy land.

A butterfly wore stripes so wild,
It fluttered like a playful child.
I chased it down through twirls and twangs,
But tripped on roots, and made some clangs.

The sun dipped low, a cheeky grin,
As I landed in a patch of spin.
Grass laughed softly at my fall,
Nature's humor, it pleased us all.

Dreams danced 'neath a swirling sky,
As nightfall wrapped with a sleepy sigh.
We winked at stars and gently swayed,
In dappled dreams, where laughter played.

Histories Written in Bark

The trees are scribes of funny tales,
With carved initials of lovers' fails.
Each mark a giggle, every notch,
A secret shared in nature's watch.

A raccoon pondered life and snacks,
While plotting his next daring hacks.
He stacked some acorns, made a throne,
Declared this kingdom all his own.

Old branches creaked with laughter loud,
At chips of wood that puffy crowd.
They whispered tales of days long past,
Where mischief lived and shadows cast.

With every bark a story spins,
Of playful winds and joyful grins.
Nature's history, trite and light,
In twisted roots, we found delight.

Leaves That Dance in Silence

The leaves sway gently, quite the show,
A whispered giggle, the breeze will blow.
They tango and twist in a leafy cheer,
But shh! Not a soul knows what they hear.

The squirrels laugh, they scout the scene,
Dressed in acorns, they feel so clean.
They pirouette 'neath the branches tall,
While shadows of laughter begin to sprawl.

Nature's Lullaby in Green

In leafy cradles, the critters hum,
To nature's rhythm, they start to strum.
A melody soft, with a tickle of fun,
While hedgehogs bounce, saying, "We've just begun!"

The background chorus, a rustling thrill,
Each gust of wind, it gives a chill.
With whispers of chuckles, they softly play,
In this green concert that grows every day.

Eclipsed by the Embrace of Trees

Here comes the sun, but wait—what's this?
A shadowy figure, can't let it miss!
The tree's arms sway, like they're in the know,
While critters below dance to and fro.

With roots intertwined, they plot and scheme,
To trick the leaves into one big dream.
A circus of joy, they leap and bound,
In a leafy secret, where laughter's found.

Crystal Raindrops on Leaves

Raindrops plop, a splashy affair,
They tickle the leaves like they don't care.
Each droplet giggles, a crystal delight,
Creating a splash show, oh what a sight!

As puddles gather, skipping becomes,
The dance of the droplets, oh how it hums!
With nature as stage, and laughter up high,
This frolicsome banquet of fun in the sky.

Beneath the Boughs of Memory

Squirrels chatter in whispered glee,
As acorns tumble from the tree.
A rabbit hops, with quite the dance,
Wearing leaves, it takes a chance.

The breeze giggles, a playful tease,
Tickling branches like naughty peas.
Mistakes abound in nature's jest,
A bird on a branch, it fails the test.

Twilight hangs like a slinky's bend,
As shadows stretch and giggles blend.
Memory frolics, a carefree sprite,
Beneath the boughs, we hide our fright.

Sunlight's Kiss on Mossy Stones

Sunlight breaks, and stones do blink,
Mossy hats cause frogs to think.
A snail slides slow, in quite a race,
While lizards laugh, they set the pace.

Worms do the cha-cha, oh what a sight,
As beetles waltz into the night.
Puddles giggle, reflecting sun,
Nature's party has just begun!

The brook hums tunes, a lively jam,
While fish flash smiles, like a grand slam.
Here sunlight's kiss sparks all the fun,
It's a wild dance, we've just begun!

The Hushed Murmurs of Nature's Cloak

Leaves murmur secrets, gossip galore,
While ants parade on their tiny tour.
A fox, with style, struts through the shade,
In a bowtie made from fallen jade.

Crickets chirp in a hilarious band,
Their beatboxing skills truly unplanned.
A raccoon juggles, but drops his snack,
Giggles ripple through the forest track.

Behind each tree, the laughter grows,
With whispers sweet like nature's prose.
Life spins tales, in muted tones,
The cloak of woods, filled with funny bones.

A Tangle of Branches and Dreams

Twigs entwine like lovers bold,
In a tangle where tales unfold.
A spider spins, with quite a flair,
His web a stage for jokes to share.

The moon peeks in, a cheeky sprite,
Winking down on the giggling night.
Owls chuckle deep, in familiar chats,
As squirrels debate who's fatter—cats!

In a ruffled nest, chicks play cartoon,
While fireflies dance to a catchy tune.
Dreams take flight through a swirling breeze,
In branches tangled, laughter frees.

The Embrace of Gnarled Roots

In a tangle of roots, a squirrel makes schemes,
Dreaming of acorns, or so it seems.
With each tiny leap, he fluffs up his tail,
As he plans his great heist on a neighboring snail.

A worm pokes his head, with a look of disdain,
"What's with the fuss? It's all such a pain!"
The squirrel just laughs, with a tilt of his hat,
"I'll be rich in no time, don't be such a brat!"

Beneath the Treetops' Embrace

Under the branches, a party unfolds,
With raccoons and rabbits, both daring and bold.
They gather for snacks, a feast on the ground,
While a wise old owl hoots, "Hey, look what I found!"

A pie made of nuts, with berries so sweet,
The animals cheer, "Oh, what a treat!"
But the raccoon's plan to take it all home,
Ends with him stuck in a green sticky foam.

A Tapestry of Leaf and Light

Leaves dance in the breeze, a colorful sight,
While a chubby beetle rolls in sheer delight.
He trips on a twig, goes flying afar,
"Was that a leaf, or a near-miss with a car?"

The sunlight chuckles, spills laughter along,
As the beetle recovers, he hums a new song.
The trees join the tune with their rustling cheer,
While the beetle insists, "I'm the star of the year!"

Reveries in the Thicket

In a cozy thicket where giggles collide,
A hedgehog throws parties, and everyone hides.
With his spikes all a-shimmer, he calls, "Don't be shy!
If you're brave, come play and give it a try!"

A shy little mouse, peeks out with a grin,
But tumbles and rolls, ending up in the bin.
As laughter erupts, he blushes quite red,
"Next time I'll bring cheese, but no more bread!"

Enchantment in the Shade

In whispers soft, the branches sway,
The squirrels dance, come out to play.
A buzzing bee, in stripes of gold,
    Giggles echo, secrets told.

The sunlight spills like melted cheese,
While ants march on, as if at ease.
With every rustle, laughter flows,
The trees might hide, but never doze.

A hat atop a hedgehog's head,
"Hey, look at me!" it bravely said.
The rabbits laugh, they join the fun,
In this wild world, we all are one.

So come on in, you silly friends,
Where nature's joy and humor blends.
In shadows deep, let laughter bloom,
Within the shade, there's always room.

Children of the Woodlands

With sticks in hand, they roam around,
A kingdom built upon the ground.
They laugh and shout, a wild parade,
In leafy forts, their dreams are made.

A bird that sings, a frog that croaks,
They mimic sounds, these woodland folks.
With every leap and bound they take,
They stumble, trip, and laugh — oh, what a break!

A branch that cracks, a sudden squeak,
They freeze in place, not wanting to peek.
But then, a giggle breaks the spell,
And all bursts forth, a joyous yell.

The wildflowers wear crowns of green,
As little kings and queens convene.
They crown the toad, the noble sage,
And dance around their forest stage.

Beneath the Canopy's Watch

In shades of green, they plot and scheme,
Beneath the trees, they chase a dream.
With a cap of leaves and shoes of mud,
They leap right into a squishy flood.

The shadows dance, the sunlight winks,
They giggle hard, with happy clinks.
A playful breeze gives leafy cheers,
As laughter rings, it drowns out fears.

A raccoon peeks from behind a tree,
"Not a thief!" it claims, "Just come to see!"
The children roar with joyous glee,
As mud pies fly, a sight to see.

Within the wild, their voices blend,
In every corner, joy can mend.
So let them play, let spirits soar,
Beneath the watch of branches' lore.

The Duality of Light and Shade

In shadows long, the giggles echo,
A game of hide-and-seek in meadow.
A sunny smile, a cheeky glance,
The sunbeams leap, they start to dance.

Oh, what a place to spin around,
Where sunshine plays upon the ground.
The blades of grass tickle the toes,
As whispers pass through the gentle throes.

But darkness hides its playful grin,
Where not a light can creep within.
The thrill of fright on a moonlit trail,
A spooky laugh, a true fairy tale.

Then back to light, they tumble free,
In this arena, pure jubilee.
With every shade, a new surprise,
Life's funny tricks are in disguise.

Enchantment in the Green Wilds.

In the woods where squirrels play,
Giggles echo in the day.
Frogs wear crowns made out of grass,
While dancing ants form a class.

Bumblebees with tiny hats,
Boogie with the chubby rats.
Trees nod as they tell a joke,
Even mushrooms laugh and poke.

Butterflies flap with such grace,
Turning flowers into a race.
Rabbits in sunglasses prance,
Inviting all to join the dance.

Whispers of the Canopy

Chatter of leaves is quite the treat,
They gossip about who's got big feet.
When the breeze blows, trees start to sway,
Making jokes throughout the day.

Caterpillars wear silly frowns,
As they inch through leafy towns.
Covered in fuzz, not a care in sight,
They hope for wings to take flight.

Old owls hoot in a rhythmic rhyme,
Wishing they could freeze all time.
But when a squirrel tells a tale,
Even they crack up without fail.

Shadows Beneath the Boughs

Shadows leap and skip around,
They tell secrets without a sound.
Trees stretch their limbs with a grin,
Hiding giggles underneath their skin.

In this wild and wacky land,
You'll find a rabbit in a band.
With carrots strummed like a ukulele,
He sings tunes that surely sway me.

Mice in shoes glide to the beat,
Making each dance-off quite a feat.
Even the crickets join the parade,
Creating music that never fades.

Dance of the Forest Spirits

In the glade where dreams collide,
Spirits meet with laughter wide.
They twirl in circles, full of cheer,
Chasing shadows, drawing near.

With leaf-crowns perched on their heads,
They leap over patches and beds.
Mocking the owls who blink twice,
As their jig turns exquisite and nice.

Fireflies light up the scene,
Creating a disco that's unseen.
Each flicker a twinkling delight,
Under the stars, they dance all night.

Eves of Enchanted Forests

In dusk's embrace, the critters dance,
Chipmunks in hats, they take a chance.
With acorn-tossing skills that amaze,
They chat and giggle in leafy bays.

The squirrels plot their grand heist spree,
To swipe a snack from a buzzing bee.
While owls wear glasses to read the score,
Of tales untold from folklore galore.

Beneath the branches, laughter soars,
As fireflies play in sparkling floors.
A raccoon complains, "Where's my dessert?"
While frogs in coats still plan to flirt.

The moon peeks in with a cheeky grin,
As pixies twirl, letting the fun begin.
In magic's hold, the mischief thrives,
In enchanted woods, where silliness dives.

Linger in the Lush

In vibrant shades, the jester trees,
Wave their branches in springtime breeze.
With mossy hats and shoes of bark,
They dance around, making their mark.

A group of rabbits plays hopscotch wide,
While turtles race with humor as their guide.
A mockingbird sings an off-key tune,
As hedgehogs waltz beneath the moon.

The breeze whispers secrets to the grass,
Tickling the leaves as the critters pass.
In shadows cast by the sunlit spires,
A show unfolds that never tires.

With giggles echoing through the grove,
It's where the playful spirits rove.
So linger on in the vibrant throng,
For laughter blooms, and nothing's wrong.

Sunbeams Through Emerald Canopies

The sunlight sprinkles like confetti bright,
As ants march in line, what a silly sight!
A squirrel on a skateboard rides the breeze,
Flipping nuts as he giggles with ease.

With spiderwebs strung like a party's flair,
Caught up in traps, the flies unaware.
While laughter rings from the shades above,
Under the leaves, there's mischief to love.

The daisies dance in a conga line,
While bees join in with buzz and whine.
In dappled light, fun never wanes,
With wildflower schemes that brighten our brains.

As shadows blend, a creature peeks,
With tiny eyes and muddy cheeks.
What fun it is to murmur and shout,
In the leafy realm where spirits flout.

A Solace in the Leafy Mirth

Beneath the sky of giddy blue,
The trees wear smiles; yes, it's true!
A pillow of grass with laughter sewn,
In leafy embrace, we feel at home.

Chipmunks joke about rainy days,
While a wise old turtle nods and sways.
Creating chaos with joyful leaps,
In the leafy mirth, fun never sleeps.

The shadows weave through the playful ground,
Tickling feet with their soft surround.
Amid the whispers of a gentle breeze,
Laughter springs, and troubles freeze.

So come and join this woodland song,
In the leafy laughter where we belong.
With each soft rustle, we share a cheer,
In this heartfelt realm where all draw near.

The Language of Leaves Unfurled

The leaves dance merry in the sun,
They whisper secrets, just for fun.
One leaf says, 'I'd love to float!'
The other giggles, 'Oh, just note!'

Squirrels debate the best acorn,
In the shade, where chatter's born.
A gust whooshes, they take flight,
Stumbling around, what a sight!

A crow caws loudly, makes it clear,
Perhaps he's drunk on cherry beer.
The branches sway with tipsy grace,
Leaves chuckle at this raucous race.

In nature, humor seems to thrive,
Even when the trees arrive.
So hear them laughing, don't be shy,
Join in their fun, just give a try!

Reveries Beneath the Silent Trees

A tree's thick bark is quite a hoot,
It sways and shakes in its own suit.
Roots wiggle like a happy worm,
While talking leaves just love to squirm.

A raccoon tells a sunlit tale,
Of midnight snacks and pizza pale.
The mossy floor, a laughing stage,
Each old stump holds a wise old page.

The owls wink with sneaky glee,
As shadows dance right next to me.
The branches whisper soft and low,
'Keep it secret — we all know!'

So join this club of leafy cheer,
Wear a crown of twigs, my dear.
Beneath these trees, let humor spill,
Nature's jesters bring the thrill!

Sketches in the Shade

In the shade where the colors play,
Leaves draw pictures, bright as day.
One shows a cat that walks on air,
The others giggle, 'What a flare!'

A beetle struts with pompous flair,
While ants march past without a care.
They stumble over twigs and stones,
Making art with all their bones.

The grass whispers, 'Watch the show!'
As butterflies flit to and fro.
One takes a tumble, oh what fun,
Painting chaos in the sun.

So gather round with eyes so wide,
In the shade, let laughter bide.
With crayons made from worldly sights,
Sketch out joy beneath the heights!

Echoing Footfalls Through the Grove

Footfalls echo, what a sound,
In the grove, it spins around.
A squirrel trips, oh what a fall,
Then jumps up high, just like a ball.

See that owl with glasses thick?
He watches all in one quick flick.
Hoo laughs at shoes lost to the tree,
Where branches tickle legs with glee.

As shadows stretch and giggles wave,
The tiny paths behave like brave.
The grass beneath sings tales so loud,
Time for a prank — I'm so proud!

So take a stroll, let laughter rise,
In this grove, find sweet surprise.
With each footfall, nature's call,
Brings smiles to one and all!

Dance of the Leafy Sentinels

In the breeze, they shimmy and sway,
Twirling with laughter, they'd dance all day.
Branches whisper secrets, oh what a sight,
Wiggling their toes in the warm sunlight.

Squirrels join in, with a flip and a twist,
Chasing their shadows, they just can't resist.
While birds are singing, the leaves join the fun,
Creating a chaos, oh what a run!

Each gust a giggle, each tremor a jest,
Nature's own party, the very best fest.
Frogs hop along, making quite the parade,
While critters are plotting their grand escapade.

So when you stroll by, just take a peek,
At the leafy crew, it's laughter they seek.
Under the sun, they spin and they fling,
Join in their antics, let your heart sing!

Echoes in the Thicket

In the thickets, voices rise,
Chit-chats of critters, what a surprise!
Bunnies gossip, while foxes retort,
Squirrels are jesting, quite the support.

A badger rolls over, giggling aloud,
While the owls hoot softly, proud of their crowd.
Mice share their tales of the cheese they stole,
Each laugh a whisper, a playful scroll.

Through rustling leaves, stories fly,
Echoes of laughter, a comical sigh.
Nature's own soap opera, wild and spry,
With every new twist, the punchline's nearby.

As dusk approaches, the antics slow down,
Animals yawn, wearing sleep like a crown.
But in the thicket, new tales still bloom,
Waiting for dawn to awaken the room!

Beneath the Green Tapestry

Under the leaves, a stage is set,
Where laughter and mischief haunt every pet.
The ants march in rhythm, a comical line,
Each step a giggle, oh, isn't it fine?

Beetles rolling acorns, what a surprise,
Their tiny parade, a feast for the eyes.
While butterflies flutter like confetti in air,
Whispering jokes without a single care.

In shadows they plot a caper or two,
With witty retorts, they'd know what to do.
The crows are the judges, with caws loud and clear,
Rendering verdicts on each funny cheer.

Beneath the green, where laughter runs free,
A world of amusement awaits you and me.
So come for a visit, share in the fun,
With giggles and glee, until the day's done!

Conversations with Sylvan Shadows

Shadows in trees, they whisper and tease,
Glancing at passersby with the slightest of ease.
Each dappled light holds a giggling friend,
Their chatter a soundtrack that never will end.

Mushrooms debate on the best rain to fall,
While ferns listen closely, they giggle and sprawl.
Curly vines wrap around, joining the chat,
Pagans of humor, oh, imagine that!

Soft breezes carry the punchlines around,
Even the rocks chuckle without making a sound.
While crickets drum up the rhythm to sway,
The shadows keep laughing, come join the ballet!

As stars start to twinkle, the moon makes a face,
The shadows keep chattering, a wild embrace.
So sit back a moment, let joy be your guide,
In this leafy venue, let laughter abide!

Forest Guardians in Twilight

In the hush of dimming light,
The owls hoot, oh what a sight!
Squirrels in capes, they dance and twirl,
While rabbits play tag and whirl.

Raccoons wear masks, quite the affair,
Stumbling through foliage without a care.
A bear in pajamas steals a snack,
As critters gather, no one holds back.

Fireflies flicker, their lanterns bright,
As trees gossip under the night.
"Did you see the hedgehog's new hat?"
The forest chuckles at that chitchat.

So here in twilight, laughter blends,
Where trees stand tall and joy transcends.
With whiskers twitching, and tails in sway,
The forest guardians hold sway.

Soliloquy of the Twisted Trunks

Oh twisted trunks, with stories to share,
Confessions of squirrels, who can't help but stare.
A woodpecker's drum gets the fun parade,
While rabbits poke fun at how the trees swayed.

In secret whispers, the branches delight,
Telling each other who's who in the night.
"I heard the fox tried to catch a hare,"
And giggles erupt in the cool evening air.

The old oak claims wisdom, but falls for a joke,
As vines wrap around him, his pride they choke.
With snickers and snorts, the grove comes alive,
Where nature's own jesters expertly thrive.

So listen, dear friend, to this uproarious scene,
Where bark's full of giggles and leaves shimmy green.
The trunks, though twisted, find joy in their stance,
In the laughter of nature, they happily dance.

Songs in the Breeze

The wind whistles tunes through branches and leaves,
As chipmunks prance, no one believes.
A songbird croons, quite off-key,
While the critters join in, full of glee.

A deer with flair does a silly jig,
His friends clap hooves, just a bit too big.
With rustling laughter, the treetops sway,
In this musical show, all join the play.

The breeze carries whispers of funny debate,
Who's the best dancer? "I think it's the mate!"
A hedgehog in tutu prances around,
As butterflies giggle without making a sound.

So sing with the wind, let joy take its flight,
In the heart of the woods, everything feels right.
Where tunes make the trees sway, soft laughter resounds,
Life's a grand concert in these verdant grounds.

Beneath Verdant Arches

Beneath the arches of emerald green,
Frogs in tuxedos strut with keen.
They croak out riddles, quite absurd,
While dragonflies buzz, not a single word.

Twigs tap dance, like they've got the groove,
As the sun dips low, they start to move.
With mischief afoot, the bushes shake,
While ants form a train for a pie to bake.

Chirping crickets bring beat to the night,
While a slow snail joins, what a sight!
"Why race?" he grumbles, "I take my time!"
And the crowd bursts out in giggles sublime.

So here's to the frolics beneath the bright boughs,
Where nature's a jester, and laughter allows,
With whimsy and fun in every small space,
It's a comical world, a delightful embrace.

Echoes Through the Green

The squirrels play hide and seek,
With acorns as their prize,
But when they trip on a twig,
Oh, how laughter fills the skies!

A bird gets tangled in a dance,
With leaves that swirl and sway,
She struts like she owns the place,
Until she flies the wrong way!

A rabbit hops with such delight,
Chasing shadows in the breeze,
He stops to ponder daisies bright,
Then sneezes, echoing through trees!

The sun dips low, it's time to play,
With fireflies spelling "cheese,"
As nature's laughter fills the air,
In this quirky, leafy tease!

Secrets in Sunlit Glades

The fox unveils his finest trick,
Wearing a hat made of grass,
He prances 'round, all sly and slick,
While giggles from the past still pass.

A tortoise with a tiny cart,
Sells cookies baked by cheer,
But each customer takes the part,
Of jesters knocking with good cheer!

Beneath a bough, a raccoon sings,
His notes are quite the mess,
He hopes for treats on silver strings,
And ends with a comical guess!

The shadows stretch as day departs,
With echoes sweetly near,
These secrets of the glade in parts,
Bring chuckles we all cheer!

Rustling Tales of the Woodland

The deer wear glasses, quite absurd,
Reading maps that they have made,
But every turn leads to a bird,
Who says, "You're lost, I'm afraid!"

The mushrooms whisper jokes on roots,
About the flowers still in bloom,
While ants on tiny bustling hoots,
Bring laughter to the gloomy gloom!

A bear attempts to bake a pie,
Using honey, leaves, and pine,
But ends up making bee-wings fly,
With giggles filled, all's just fine!

In rustling tales where fun prevails,
The woodland spirits beam,
With myth and mirth in all their trails,
They weave a joyful dream!

Murmurs of the Verdant Veil

The breeze hums softly through the leaves,
Tickling noses, making sneeze,
While lizards wear their best green sleeves,
Strutting with the greatest ease!

A hedgehog stars in his own show,
Rolling down a grassy hill,
He's the king of folly, don't you know?
With squeaks that thrill and spill!

Two owls debate 'til late at night,
About who's wisest of them all,
One says, "I took flight at first light!"
The other says, "You're just small!"

In murmurs that the creatures share,
The verdant veil is full of cheer,
With every laugh hanging in air,
And joyfulness is all we hear!

Serenity in the Canopy's Embrace

In the shade, the squirrels play,
Chasing shadows, bright as day.
A chipmunk sings a silly song,
While the wise old owl hoots along.

Branches wiggle in the breeze,
The sun peeks through with playful tease.
A leaf drops down; it makes a sound,
A funny dance across the ground.

Raccoons wear masks like they're jesters,
Sneaking snacks like forest testers.
They jive and shimmy under the spray,
Of laughing sunlight, come what may.

Nature's giggles fill the air,
As breezes tickle without a care.
In this bliss, let's join the cheer,
For every whisper, brings us near.

The Poetry of Rustling Leaves

Whispers echo in the trees,
The leaves are gossiping with ease.
They crackle jokes and share a laugh,
As branches draft the silliest half.

A leaf floats down, a graceful waltz,
It lands upon a frog, who exalts!
Jumping up, he takes a bow,
While ladybugs cheer him, 'Wow!'

The busy ants are running late,
Deciding if it's fun or fate.
Their tiny voices, full of glee,
Declare, 'Let's race! 1-2-3!'

The canopy sings a merry tune,
Beneath the watchful eye of the moon.
Each rustle reminds us to be bright,
In nature's theater, pure delight.

Veins of the Forest Heart

Twisting vines, like playful kids,
On the forest floor, where mischief bids.
They tug and pull, a lively fight,
Their laughter rings through day and night.

The ferns don hats like dapper folk,
While mushrooms giggle, bright and woke.
"Let's have a party!" shouts the moss,
A celebration of nature, no loss.

A wandering rabbit hops on scene,
Pausing to fix his collar, keen.
He bows to trees, so tall and grand,
And leads the dance, a funny band.

In this kingdom of leafy green,
Every heartbeat bursts with sheen.
The forest winks, a mischievous start,
With veins of laughter, the forest's heart.

Where Light Meets Lushness

Sunshine tickles the ground below,
Where playful shadows dance in tow.
The leafy crowns wear beams like crowns,
As sunlight twirls in leafy gowns.

Butterflies, the jesters bright,
Flit and flutter with sheer delight.
They tease the flowers, 'Do you see?'
A giggle grows in jubilee.

A tiny beetle, dressed in style,
Struts along with a confident smile.
He winks at bees who buzz with flair,
A comedy act beyond compare.

Where warmth and greenery intertwine,
Nature delivers her punchline.
We'll laugh and play, come take a chance,
In this cheerful, leafy dance.

The Heart of the Whispering Woods

Squirrels gossip in the trees,
Their chatter floats upon the breeze.
A rabbit hops, a punchline delivered,
And with each jump, the forest quivered.

The owls hoot jokes in the dark,
They search for laughs like a quirky lark.
With every rustle, a giggle stirs,
Nature's jesters in fuzzy furs.

A deer slips on leaves, such a clumsy sight,
While frogs leap about, playing tag at night.
The sun sneezes gold, through branches it peeks,
Life in the woods is a riddle that speaks.

Laughter echoes, a woodland tune,
As critters dance beneath the moon.
In every shadow, a cheeky grin,
In this calm chaos, we all fit in.

Flickers of Sunlit Dreams

Bumblebees buzz with a silly song,
Dancing through petals, where they belong.
Butterflies giggle, flitting about,
In a fluttering race, there's never a doubt.

The sunbeams play hide and seek with the clouds,
While foxes wear masks, feeling quite proud.
A raccoon juggles acorns for fun,
With every drop, the squirrels would run.

The shadows cast playful figures at dusk,
As chipmunks make trick-or-treat a must.
Nature's a stage, it's a sight to see,
A comedy show, wild and free.

Laughter wraps 'round like a vibrant vine,
Each creature adds a punchline so fine.
In this whimsical world, a dream takes flight,
Sparking joy in the soft twilight.

Beneath the Shelter of Branches

Under the canopy, whispers abound,
As clever little critters scuttle around.
A hedgehog rolls, tired of his prickle,
While even the ants get caught in a giggle.

The shadows play tricks, a playful charade,
Where leaves tell tales of the pranks they made.
A woodpecker knocks a rhythm so bold,
It's a concert of nature, a story retold.

Sunbeams peek in with a mischievous grin,
Lighting up pathways where adventures begin.
The roots of the trees hold secrets and dreams,
With laughter that ripples like babbling streams.

Every rustle and flutter invites the delight,
Spinning yarns that tickle the stars at night.
In this patch of magic, where the funny sings,
We find joy in the simplest things.

The Dance of the Falling Leaves

Leaves twirl down in a dizzy parade,
Each one a dancer, unafraid.
They spin and they tumble, a colorful show,
Performing for critters who watch from below.

A chipmunk does tricks, teasing the wind,
While a crow caws laughter, feeling quite grinned.
With every mayfly that buzzes its tune,
Nature's own comedy, bright as the moon.

In puddles of sunlight, reflections of cheer,
Swaying to melodies only they hear.
Gathering memories, the colors collide,
A whimsical dance with laughter as guide.

Together they twinkle, a playfull refrain,
In silken cascades, like soft summer rain.
As the night gently falls, they giggle away,
In this merry ballet, the world starts to sway.

Footprints on the Soft Moss

Froggy leaps and splashes, oh so spry,
With a skip and a hop, he catches the eye.
Squirrels gossip 'bout the shoes left behind,
Were they big or were they small, let's see what we find.

Beneath the tall trees, a dance floor in green,
The raccoons start a party, oh what a scene!
A lost sandal, a discarded old hat,
Whispers of laughter ring out, just like that.

Fungi boot prints, looking quite grand,
Tell tales of mischief throughout the land.
Who wore them last? Was it you or your cat?
One thing's for sure, they're not for a brat!

In this soft moss, where stories reside,
Each footprint a giggle, each laugh is our guide.
Frogs croon a lullaby under the night,
As the moon laughs along, with its silvery light.

Tales of Time in the Timber

Where woodpeckers peck, and the squirrels steal snacks,
Time shimmies like a dancer, no signs of laid backs.
A turtle winks at the trees standing tall,
As bugs dress in bowties, having a ball.

Old trunks tell secrets, wrapped tight as a drum,
Creaking and cracking, oh, don't be so glum!
Each ring a reminder of silly old tales,
Of raccoons in tuxedos, executing their trails.

Even the wind chuckles, brushing through leaves,
Carrying giggles and playful reprieves.
The shadows feel ticklish, as sunbeams collide,
In a timeless embrace, no reason to hide.

Every creature whispers, no need to shout,
In tales of the timber, there's joy all about.
So let's sit on this moss, and share in the cheer,
For laughter, my friend, is what brings us all near.

The Heartbeat of the Quiet Grove

The gentle heartbeat, of this curious space,
A bunny hops by, in a comical race.
With a wiggle of nose, and a flick of its ears,
It bounds with a joy, that quiets our fears.

A wise old owl hoots, with a wink in its eye,
"Why do squirrels juggle acorns?" we sigh.
The laughter of trees, in whispers and rustles,
As wind plays a tune, and the world gently tussles.

The beetle brigade, in a marching parade,
With tiny drumsticks, they've come to invade.
They laugh at the thought of a grand old debate,
"Who's faster, the snail or this fella on fate?"

In this woodsy heart, where the silence is sweet,
Every chuckle and giggle is a rhythmic heartbeat.
The calm wraps around, like a warm, fuzzy cloak,
In the quiet grove, humor's easy to poke.

Harmony in Hushed Corners

In corners where whispers settle and sway,
A trio of frogs begins their cabaret.
With a leap and a croak, they steal the spotlight,
As crickets tap dance in the soft moonlight.

Under twinkling stars, shadows sway and twist,
A raccoon brings popcorn, can't let it be missed!
A gathering of creatures, all woven in fun,
Under the leafy canopy, they bask in the sun.

Foxes in tuxedos, so dashing and spry,
Try a little jig, oh my, oh my!
As owls hoot along, with a wise, quirky grin,
This harmony sings of the sillies within.

So raise a glass of dew, let the laughter roll,
In these hushed corners, we discover our soul.
Nature's comedy plays on an eternal stage,
With every rustle and giggle, we flip to the next page.

The Call of the Woodland Creatures

A squirrel danced in his best attire,
With acorns hidden, his secret desire.
The owl hooted loud, preparing to jest,
While rabbits debated which lettuce is best.

The raccoons wore masks, a bandit parade,
As hedgehogs rolled in their spiky charade.
They threw a grand feast, with mushrooms and cheese,
Under the canopy, swaying with ease.

A fox told a joke, and the trees all shook,
While deer chuckled softly, tucked under the nook.
Each critter was merry, caught up in the fun,
In laughter they thrived, 'til the day was done.

So if you wander where sunlight beams,
Listen for giggles that dance through your dreams.
The woodland's alive, it's a raucous affair,
With creatures so silly, they simply don't care.

Journey Through the Swaying Branches

With a hop and a skip, the squirrel takes flight,
Stealing a glance at the bird's morning plight.
The branches are swaying, a playful ballet,
As critters perform in their own wacky way.

The raccoon rolls down, through leaves and the muck,
Mumbling and grumbling, 'Oh, what's my luck?'
While the blue jay squawks, with news to get right,
'They say there's a party—come join us tonight!'

A hedgehog on stilts tries to greet the sun,
But trips on a twig, oh what silly fun!
The trees just laughed, 'Ah, what a sight!'
As frolicsome critters embraced the daylight.

So join in the dance, let your spirit fly,
Through breezy avenues where laughter defies.
Under the green canopy, life is a tease,
Every twist and turn's a new chance to please.

Lyricals of the Old Growth

In the heart of the forest, the old trees hum,
With tales of their youth, when they were so dumb.
A bear tunes his voice, it's a very bad note,
But still all the critters sway, cheer, and gloat.

The wise old owl chuckles, perched high with pride,
'Oh, dear friends, remember when you said, "Let's glide?"

Then fell on your tails and got stuck in the brambles,
Creating a ruckus with comical rambles?'

With every old leaf, there's a story or two,
Of mischief and laughter, both old and new.
The mushrooms provide shade for the tales to unfold,
Where giggles ring out, and bright colors are bold.

So wander the woods, where the jesters convene,
In thickets and thorns, where life's rarely mean.
For here in the green, there's magic and jest,
And laughter entwined in the forest's sweet quest.

Conversations with the Wind

The wind whistled through leaves with a cheeky refrain,
'Tell me your secrets, I'll keep them plain!'
A raccoon said, 'Wind, let's whisper our dreams,
I wanted to dance with the light of moonbeams!'

The breeze laughed aloud, rustling playful and spry,
Returning with stories that tickled the sky.
'What's this about dancing? Let's throw a grand ball,
Invite all the critters—just give me a call!'

A fox jumped up high, his tail trailing wide,
'Let's make it a party, where everyone's tried!'
While trees swayed in rhythm, all brushed by the gust,
The woodland erupted, oh, fun was a must!

So follow the wind, let your laughter run free,
Join the woodland chat, let your heart fill with glee.
For under the stars, where nothing's amiss,
Conversations abound in a magical bliss.

Threads of Gold in the Wildlife

Squirrels chat in winter coats,
While bears nap, making silly notes.
A fox sneezes in blooming rays,
Who knew he'd share those sunny days?

Hares race down the winding trail,
A turtle grins, 'You'll never prevail!'
A dance of paws, a whirl of fur,
Nature's giggles softly purr.

Birds boast of their latest tricks,
While frogs croak in rhythmic picks.
The laughter echoes from the stream,
Where everything is just a dream.

So visit this patch of mirth and cheer,
Where every creature whispers near.
With threads of gold stitching the skies,
Wildlife's humor never dies.

Beneath the Vaulted Green

Under a canopy of leafy laughs,
A raccoon digs up some old photographs.
The sun shines down, a playful tease,
As ants debate the mysteries of cheese.

Monkeys chatter, pulling pranks,
While frogs play cards beside the banks.
A tale of tricks, a jest or two,
Stars start to giggle, what a view!

The shadows dance, the breezes play,
A squirrel's joke brightens the day.
Branches swaying, what a sight,
As nature's children laugh with delight.

So here in green where laughter steeps,
Life's funny secrets the forest keeps.
Beneath the vaulted sanctuary,
A comedy unfolds, wild and merry.

Traces of Time Underbrush

In thickets thick with tales untold,
Lies a hedgehog who's slightly too bold.
He wears a hat made from an acorn,
Declaring, 'I'm the king, forlorn!'

A stray leaf chases a careless breeze,
While a woodpecker plays with his keys.
Wind whispers secrets from days gone by,
And clouds float by, the giggling sky.

An old owl hoots, wise and strange,
Even he finds these antics deranged.
'What's pranking now?' he starts to muse,
In the underbrush, nobody snooze!

With every rustle, a chuckle's spawned,
As beetles dance to a tune they've spawned.
In the traces of time, joy's the call,
Laughing under the trees, we share it all.

The Poetry of Stillness

In quietude, the whispers play,
Where slumbering mice dream the day away.
A stone rolls by, what a surprise,
And crickets join in chorus, oh my!

The brook chuckles as it flows,
Tickling senses in rhythmic prose.
Here even silence has a jest,
With shadows flitting, nature's best.

A sleepy owl gives an eye-roll,
As bushes burst out with laughter whole.
Even the hush holds something fun,
Life's cozy jokes for everyone.

So sit awhile, breathe in the air,
Listen closely; laughter is everywhere.
In the poetry of stillness lies,
The comic quirk that never dies.

A Palette of Autumn Hues

The trees are dressed in a vibrant gown,
With swirls of orange and shades of brown.
Squirrels ride bikes, so clever and spry,
While acorns fall down like pies from the sky.

The pumpkins grinned wide, adorned like clowns,
As leaves twirled and danced, wearing their crowns.
A fluttering joke, they whisper with glee,
"Why is the tree always so happy?" "Cause it's free!"

The wind joins the laughter, a playful breeze,
Tickling the branches, teasing the leaves.
A chorus of chuckles fills up the air,
As nature's own jesters perform without care.

In every bright color, there's joy to be found,
The forest is laughing, a riotous sound.
So grab all your friends, come join in the fun,
In this vibrant tale, autumn's just begun!

Nature's Soft Serenade

The brook sings sweetly, a melody near,
While frogs form a band, playing without fear.
A moonlit waltz in the darkening wood,
Where critters are crooning, it's quite understood.

The crickets tap dance on mossy old logs,
And owls hoot the verses, no room for snogs.
With raccoons as dancers, they twirl with grace,
Inventing new dances, a comical space.

The trees sway and giggle, a bow here and there,
As shadows embrace, adding rhythm to air.
"What's the best dance?" they chat with a laugh,
"Why, the jig of the beetles—in half and half!"

Under soft starlight, the symphony grows,
With laughter and chirps, and amusing to-dos.
Nature hums softly, a tune full of cheer,
Inviting all creatures to come gather near.

Starlit Secrets of the Grove

Beneath twinkling stars, the secrets unfold,
Each leaf has a story, if only it's told.
Bunnies are gossiping, sharing the news,
While hedgehogs take bets in their little old shoes.

A squirrel is rapping, with nuts in a beat,
While badgers are grooving, swift on their feet.
The night is alive with a mystical hue,
As whispers of laughter drift softly on dew.

"What happens at dusk when the sun says goodbye?"
"The critters all come out to dance and to try!"
With lighthearted spirits, they twirl round the trees,
Inventing wild tales carried by the breeze.

The trees stand as witnesses, nodding with glee,
To secrets revealed in the dark canopy.
So listen up close as shadows collide,
For laughter and stories go hand in hand wide!

The Language of the Leaves

In whispers and rustles, the leaves share a joke,
A rendezvous planned where fun's never broke.
"Hey, did you hear? The branches will sway,
For a leaf-celebration, hip-hip-hooray!"

Colorful gossip travels on a breeze,
As leaves flap their stories with such graceful ease.
"Why do we hang out by sunlight and shade?
To sip on the whispers that autumn has made!"

With laughter echoing, a soft gentle tease,
They tickle the air and sway with the trees.
"What's one leaf's advice for another tonight?
Just let go of worries, and dance till it's light!"

So join in their chatter, that fun-filled refrain,
As leaves share their tales in the soft, golden rain.
In a world made of colors, laughter's the key,
Where every small rustle sings merrily free!

www.ingramcontent.com/pod-product-compliance
Lightning Source LLC
Chambersburg PA
CBHW071820160426
43209CB00003B/143